Praise for Reconciliation 101

"We have far too few resources at actual places and divides. What are the practices by which communities have found the ability and grace to practice and live reconciliation? This resource fills a critical gap by teaching how to form reconcilers."

- Chris Rice, Co-Director of the Duke Center for Reconciliation and author of *Grace Matters*

"Alvin has put together a readable exhortation for those who are trying to engage in the process of reconciliation. His stories and examples resonate with many of the struggles experienced by our emerging multiracial society. This handbook is a must-read primer for those seeking the basic knowledge to get started on their journey."

- Dr. George Yancey, Sociologist and author of *Beyond Racial Gridlock*

"Dr. Alvin Sanders has provided a needed resource for EFCA churches and the evangelical community in general. Too often in the church, matters of diversity and racial reconciliation are relegated to "annual event" status and not given much thought until the next year's special Sunday. This practical handbook will empower Christian leaders to teach and model the biblical values of cultural diversity, unity, and justice in the church— and to make them an ongoing part of their congregations and ministries."

–Edward Gilbreath, author of *Reconciliation Blues* and editor of UrbanFaith.com

"Alvin Sanders is a leader of leaders who knows what it means to stand in the gap between cultures. He has been bridging the divide in tough places for many years. Reconciliation is not something we can do by ourselves. We need one another. I'm grateful for Alvin who continues to lead me on this journey of understanding."

- Arloa Sutter, Breakthrough Urban Ministries

"As a pastor of a multi-cultural church with predominately an Asian American base, we sometimes don't know how to engage with the larger question of reconciliation. Alvin engages all believers regardless of ethnicity and gender to go back to the Scriptures as our authority."

- Ray Chang, Senior Pastor; Ambassador Church

"Alvin won the hearts of our Hispanic pastors the first week he came on board. Normally when Hispanics heard a discussion about reconciliation we stepped back and let the black and white brothers talk it out. But he explained how the discussion of reconciliation is not about color…it's about all of us being part of the family of God."

- Alex Mandes, EFCA Hispanic Ministries Director

"In a culture still struggling with conflict, the church needs to be part of the solution, not part of the problem. Political correctness isn't the goal, biblical correctness is; and the Bible makes it clear that reconciliation is both a missional opportunity and a theological necessity. Alvin Sanders has a unique way of helping us see that while reconciliation won't be easy, it's definitely achievable--and most of all, it pleases our Father in Heaven."

- Dr. David Faust, President; Cincinnati Christian University

"This book is an intensely practical guide to walking out reconciliation no matter what context you find yourself in. Dr. Sanders takes the conversation of reconciliation beyond black and white, demonstrating God's heart for reconciliation among ALL people as critical to the mission of Christ moving forward. This is bound to be a much-used, well-worn book in the collection of any practitioner."

- Ruth Arnold, Associate Director; 2nd Mile Ministries

"Alvin has a tremendous heart to see reconciliation become a reality and not just an ideal to which we give lip service. Best of all, I can testify to the fact that he is a man of integrity, a man that lives what he preaches."

- Paul Carpenter, Executive Pastor; Central Christian Church

"Dr. Sanders is a learned and practical man, not an ivory tower dreamer. He grasps the realities and practicalities of reconciliation up and down the ladder, from the board rooms to the interpersonal relationships. More importantly he lives what he teaches like a true man of Christ."

- Butch Ernette, Care Pastor; Hope Church

"From his heart and real life experiences as a practitioner, my Brother Alvin is providing for the Body of Christ a true gift and a workable game plan for having new conversations and deeper understanding about multicultural relations that is biblically sound and relevant to our times."

- Danté Upshaw, EFCA African-American Ministries Director

RECONCILIATION 101:
A Handbook for Ministry Leaders

ALVIN SANDERS

EFCA

Reconciliation 101: A Handbook for Ministry Leaders

Copyright © 2009 by Alvin Sanders and the Evangelical Free Church of America

Published by EFCA Publications

Distributed by:
NextStep Resources
901 East 78th Street
Minneapolis, MN 55420
www.nsresources.com
(800) 444-2665

ISBN 0-911802-35-5

Samaritan Way
901 East 78th Street
Minneapolis, MN 55420
800-745-2202
http://www.efca.org/efca-samaritan-way
samaritanway@efca.org

This book is dedicated to

Jessie and Alvin (Sr.), because of them I found success
Caroline, my bride, who has proven she can stand the rain
Hannah and Gabby, who sacrificed time with daddy
Rene' and Jessina who stick with me through thick and thin
the congregations of Hope and River of Life, who believed in me
And finally, to my EFCA family; You are a joy to serve!

Contents

A Note About Samaritan Way

In January 2008, Dr. Alvin Sanders began Samaritan Way, the reconciliation ministry of the EFCA. Overwhelmingly the most common reaction when Alvin tells people what he does is confusion. The reaction is not surprising, because this position is unique in Christian denominations.

In the EFCA, the role of the director of reconciliation is different from the secular diversity arena. The difference lies in how diversity is perceived. Instead of being an end goal, accomplishment, experience or plan, the vision is to create a network of churches that define reconciliation as the mission of God in our fallen world.

The EFCA understands that implementing the mission of *glorifying God by multiplying healthy churches among all people* is a very complex challenge for your ministry. In fact, there are very few places that you can go to get help as you develop your strategy. To help you in your journey of reconciliation, we offer several learning opportunities.

If you are interested in any of these opportunities email Alvin at samaritanway@efca.org, or call him at 800-745-2202:

Prayer Team - The EFCA has taken the unprecedented step of weaving reconciliation as the mission of God in our fallen world into the DNA of our movement. Our passion is to see our churches reverse division, multiplying kingdom growth. When it comes to reconciliation, the first step of the church in a deeply broken world is not strategy, but prayer.

Samaritan Leadership Group - A Samaritan Leadership Group is a leadership learning community on the topic of reconciliation. The group gathers to meet for a 24-hour retreat at a host site. To participate, you must be in full-time ministry.

The purpose of the gathering is to help you lead your ministry with reconciliation in mind. During the gatherings you will:

• Receive coaching on how to implement reconciliation within

your ministry
- Talk about current reconciliation leadership resources
- Analyze your ministry strategies
- Critique and pray for ministry struggles
- Build friendships with those in your district who share your passion for reconciliation

Good Samaritan Retreat - A Good Samaritan Retreat creates a learning space within your church for your leaders and members to engage reconciliation both theologically and practically. The retreat is usually done over the weekend and includes a leadership training experience for key ministry leaders one day and a sermon on the topic of reconciliation during the regularly scheduled worship service.

Sanders Leadership Consultations - This service is for ministry leaders who desire to have an in-depth assessment of their ministry concerning reconciliation issues. If your ministry is affiliated with the EFCA there is no cost. Dr. Sanders will consider ministries outside of the EFCA for a nominal fee.

Foreword

I encourage you to embrace the path of reconciliation with enthusiasm because there is little in life that I have found to compare to the depth of spiritual growth that the journey will bring.

It wasn't in the thousands of church services or Sunday school classes I attended while growing up where I first heard of the concept. Neither do I recall it even mentioned in the daily chapels or any of the numerous theological and Bible classes I took in college.

I had witnessed first-hand the riots following the death of Dr. Martin Luther King Jr. on the blocks surrounding Moody Bible Institute, where I was a student. After being awarded degrees from two venerable Christian institutions I still lacked a biblical construct that helped me put together the brokenness around me.

Rather my first introduction to the gospel explained as a message of reconciliation came from a self-described third-grade dropout; an African-American preacher named John Perkins from the most undereducated state in the union, Mississippi.

John is that rare individual that if a person has the privilege of meeting just once she or he would consider themselves blessed. I've been blessed many times, beginning when I was a young urban worker trying desperately to make sense out of the chaos of the 1960s.

When I heard John exposit Ephesians, Corinthians and numerous other passages I began to understand the source of the power of the gospel: the power to turn hate into love through the reconciling work of the cross.

His teaching rang with the authenticity born out of the crucible of life in the most racist state a person could call home. While most African-American leaders were crying "black-power," John preached reconciliation. This is incarnational love where the gospel becomes flesh.

With radical religious strife creating global threats, perhaps it is time that our churches take seriously this message of reconciliation. Has there been a better time to be an ambassador of it?

With the "browning of America" (the immigration from other countries and out-migration from cities of people of color), suburbs and small towns are experiencing previously ignored "urban" problems. If we are not going to "cut and run" from these issues, what is the answer?

It is the Word made flesh. The answer we can bring is only found in the way of the cross, the way of reconciliation, repentance and forgiveness.

It is not our accomplishments, education, giftedness or our abilities that can build bridges and mend historical pain, brokenness and alienation. It is this journey where we are all required to become wounded healers just like our Master.

I've been part of the Evangelical Free Church for almost all the forty-plus years that I journeyed this road. So, I am thrilled with this first official publication heralding our movement's commitment to build churches "among all people" by addressing reconciliation.

As a historically White/Anglo movement, we have inherited and even participated in the mistakes and injustices of the past. However, with progressive national leadership, we are now putting in place the people, process and tools that can prove to move us to be a redemptive force of the twenty-first century.

May God bless your journey as an ambassador of grace and reconciliation.

Glen Kehrein
Executive Director, Circle Urban Ministries and
Co-Author, *Breaking Down Walls*

Introduction

This guide is for ministry communities who care enough about reconciliation that they are ready to do something about it. It is especially focused toward those who are called to lead these communities.

If you picked up this book, you have probably determined that God wants you to do something in the area of reconciliation. My guess is that, at the very least, you have already started on a personal level and desire to lead your ministry in that direction, too. There are three reasons I believe I can help you on your journey.

The first stems back to April 2001, when Timothy Thomas, a 19-year-old African-American with a history of non-violent misdemeanors, was shot and killed by a Cincinnati police officer. His death caused outrage in the neighborhood of my then-church plant (River of Life), resulting in millions of dollars of damage.

It was in this environment that we held our first public worship service, in the very neighborhood that had been at the center of the rioting. River of Life became a tangible demonstration of what God can do when people from all walks of life live in unity for the advancement of the kingdom.

For seven years as the founding pastor, I was surrounded by the effects of racial, ethnic, gender, generational, and economic conflict. In leading that wonderful ministry I learned that reconciliation is a verb and is much bigger than merely achieving racial harmony between blacks and whites. I have come to believe that it is the key to fulfilling the Great Commission.

While I was at River of Life, 70 percent of those who joined had not previously had a church home. Most told me that one of the big reasons they came was the fact that everybody was accepted there, regardless of their cultural background.

Those years I spent shepherding a church in the midst of a conflicted community have made me the Christ-follower I am today. That experience has also given me a passion to spread the primary lesson I learned: that reconciliation is the mission of God in our fallen world.

The second reason I believe I can help you on your journey of reconciliation is that I have applied the principles from this handbook not only in a local church setting, but also during my stint as director of ethnic ministry at Cincinnati Christian University. While working there, I was simultaneously earning my Ph.D. I would literally write out a theory for one of my papers and then test-drive it on campus. So I am grateful to the university leadership for being my "guinea pigs." We had great success in laying the foundation for reconciliation. The faculty became integrated for the first time, and last year they experienced their biggest enrollment of ethnic students in their history.

The last reason I believe I can help you in your journey of reconciliation is because I presently serve as director of reconciliation for the Evangelical Free Church of America. Samaritan Way (the name of my ministry) was at ground zero in 2008. Now, we have successfully built a network of ministry leaders who are leading with reconciliation in mind.

I share these reasons to assure you that what you are about to read has been born in ministry *practice*. I have done some theoretical work to back up my practical suggestions, but I don't think you need much of it. You can find that elsewhere.

There are very good books on reconciliation sitting on my bookshelf. Great reads, but I will probably not revisit them. The reason is not because the books don't have relevant material. The problem lies in the fact that, typically, the books don't offer much practical help in guiding the reader to "go and do likewise," as we are told in Luke 10:37.

I would always tell my staff at River of Life, "Don't bring me a problem without offering a possible solution." That is why I have written this handbook. I have applied these principles in a church, university, and denominational setting and achieved success.

Author Henri Nouwen stated in *Reflections on Theological Education* that "writing is like giving away the loaves and fishes one has, trusting that they will multiply in the giving." My prayer is that this book will help you reverse division, multiplying kingdom growth.

Introduction

Let me offer a few tips on how to best utilize the handbook. First, as with a car owner manual, I assume you are actively driving a car. In our case, the assumption is that you are beginning your journey down the road of reconciliation. As you drive, use the principles presented to manage the dynamics of difference.

Second, I believe in the power of the *ministry community* and will use that phrase a lot. By *ministry community*, I'm referring to people who form their lives together within the context of ministry. This could be a Christian university board, church small group, or denominational staff.

These communities operate as a space where people can reflect on their experiences. As they reflect, others are allowed to offer varying viewpoints, allowing people to unearth common understanding as well as differences. Knowledge construction in the midst of relationship is what binds us together as followers of Christ. Therefore, you would be doing yourself a great disservice to read this guide alone.

You will also come across new ideas that need processing with others. So, for instance, if you are a senior pastor, read the guide with your elders as a group. Then set aside times to discuss the concepts presented.

Third, I recommend you read the chapters in order. They are based on my presentations, where I take the big picture and narrow it down to the specific. Each concept builds on the other. You could skip around, but you would probably find yourself confused if you do so.

Fourth, don't expect to find all the answers concerning reconciliation in this thin little handbook. I'm just passing along the lessons the Lord has taught me, with hope that they will move you and your ministry further down the road.

So I'll end the introduction with my bottom line, a conclusion reached from 17 years of practical ministry and academic study concerning reconciliation, and we'll build from there: The present concept of reconciliation needs to be renewed.

Read more to find out why and how to renew it.

Blessings,
Alvin Sanders
Luke 10:37

Chapter One
A Case Study - Marsha Moolah and Heath the Hick

The following is a fictional case study that is a compilation of my practical experiences in ministry. The purpose of the case study is to give you an understanding of the types of issues you may deal with as you lead with reconciliation in mind.

Her husband calls her "Marsha Moolah," because she grew up in the well-to-do suburb of Indian Hill, northeast of Cincinnati. She's always been great at academics, demonstrated by the bachelor and master degrees in education she earned at the University of Cincinnati in a five-year period.

She jokingly calls him "Heath the Hick" because of the town he is from — Hicksville! The sleepy town three hours from Cincinnati near the Ohio/Indiana border was where Heath spent his childhood. Following in the footsteps of his father, he attended Cincinnati Christian University to study for the pastorate.

Marsha and Heath first met as college seniors while they served as tutors at an inner-city elementary school. It was love at first sight and after graduation, they married.

For the first few years of their careers, both of them bounced around the Cincinnati metro, Heath as a youth pastor and Marsha as a teacher. Last year they found gold both personally and professionally.

Marsha moved from the classroom to administration by becoming principal of North College Hill Christian Academy. At the same time, Heath took on the senior pastorate of River City Church, a mere five minutes from Marsha's school.

Naturally, after landing jobs in the same community, they became intrigued by the idea of buying a house in North College Hill. They quickly found a modest three-bedroom, moved in, and began bonding with their neighbors.

But that was last year. They now are wondering what in the world they have gotten themselves into. The boards of both the church and the school have raised questions about what to do about the demographic shift taking place in North College Hill.

Fact is, as Anglos, Marsha and Heath are the minorities on their street. At most of the restaurants, gas stations, and other service industries in the neighborhood, the workers seem to be immigrants. A few low-income apartment complexes have also sprung up nearby. These trends really don't bother them.

Both Heath and Marsha have been proactive in addressing these trends — beginning by changing the organizational leadership at the church and at the Christian school. For the first time in the history of Heath's predominately Anglo church, an African-American elder (Don) has been appointed. Marsha has recruited both a business woman of Puerto Rican descent (Maria) and one of her former classmates (Dr. Liou), a second-generation Asian American, to serve on the school board.

Heath and Marsha were not prepared, though, for some of the actions and attitudes of their fellow Christians in the face of these demographic changes. The predominant responses they are seeing are negative, based on fear.

"I'm getting out while I can, while my house still has value," one of the church's former elders told Heath privately as he moved to another neighborhood. Heath also has to deal with a divided elder board concerning one of the ministry programs of Barry, his youth pastor.

Controversy / Church Change

On Sunday nights Barry plays basketball to build relationships with students. The group that shows up is becoming more and more diverse as the neighborhood changes, with fewer youth coming from families in the predominantly Anglo church. Barry has really connected with a substantial group of both low-income and non-Anglo youth through this outreach. This demographic change in who frequents the building is worrying some church members.

At Marsha's school, parents are threatening to take their kids out if the school decides to "urbanize." Mr. Phelps, a well-respected teacher, has already left to work at another school. He cited that he did not sign up to teach "those type of kids" when the board held a controversial vote over a proposal to create a diversity scholarship fund.

Controversy: Shcool Change

What is most perplexing to Heath and Marsha is that these people who are, in their opinion, acting so callously seem to be people of strong character, good intentions, and solid biblical beliefs.

The elders who are so upset about the culturally different kids coming to open gym, are they not the same ones who wanted a gym built onto the church for a sports ministry? And doesn't Mr. Phelps volunteer weekly in a poverty-stricken part of Cincinnati to tutor kids? To Heath and Marsha, it just doesn't make sense.

****

Heath calls an emergency elder-board meeting. He can feel the tension in the room. "We all know why we are here," he begins. "I want to discuss the firestorm that is brewing over Barry's open-gym policy. It seems that it has caused some people in the church to be uncomfortable."

Proponent

Various elders begin speaking up. "I don't know why," Greg says, "I was against building the gym in the first place for financial reasons, but now that I see it is bringing in unchurched kids from the neighborhood and exposing them to our ministry, I'm all for it. Isn't that what we wanted?"

Antagonist — African American

"Well yeah," Don says, "but not *all* kids. I mean, we don't want the thug element coming in and causing trouble. I went for a couple of minutes last week to see how things were going, and it looked like a hip-hop video in there! No wonder my son doesn't want to come to open gym anymore."

The elders are shocked. They were sure that an African-American would be all for keeping the open-gym policy. Heath swallows hard and asks the question everybody else is reluctant to ask: "Don, I'm not trying to be racist or disrespectful, but I'm surprised to hear that comment from you. I thought you would be pleased that open gym is drawing a lot of African-American and Latino kids."

"No offense taken, Pastor," Don replies. "Let me explain. My wife and I grew up downtown. When my wife became pregnant, we decided that we did not want to raise our children around the same negative influences we had to cope with. So we moved to North College Hill. Now I think we might have to move out farther, maybe West Chester. But we're committed to the church."

"We want our kids to go to a good school, have a nice big house, and basically experience a better quality of life. I did not go to grad school and I do not work 60-hour weeks so that my son can hang around kids like that."

"Kids like what?" Greg asks.

"Kids who are bad influences."

"How do you know they are bad influences?" Greg continues. "Have you met any of them?"

"No. But I don't have to. I grew up around them, so I know what they are about."

"I think you're unfairly labeling them as thugs," Greg gently pushes. "As far as I know, there has not been one incident of anything bad happening at open gym. In fact, my son has become good friends with Rico.

"Rico found out about our church through coming to open gym and now comes to the student small groups, on his own! He takes the bus. I've had him over for dinner, and he seems like a solid young man, the furthest thing from a thug."

Silence fills the room as Don continues to stir. *Antagonist #2*

"Well, I agree with Don," Chris says. "I mean, we all know we are to love our neighbor and be accepting of others, and we do that. I think we are a color-blind church. We have Don on our board, don't we? Rico may be O.K., but what about the others? We need some sort of policy to govern this type of thing."

"That's ridiculous!" Ray exclaims. "Are you seriously suggesting that we self-select the types of kids we allow to come to open gym?"

"Something like that," Chris replies matter-of-factly.

"That's the most ridiculous thing I've ever heard!" Ray says.

"It's not ridiculous at all," Don adds. "It's protecting our investment and the quality of our ministry."

This is going to be a long night, Heath thinks to himself.

****

This is the meeting Marsha did not want to facilitate. Last month, a heated debate took place between board members over whether to establish a scholarship program to increase both racial and economic diversity at the school.

A Case Study

Marsha saw this fund as a tool to address the developing trends of the region. Although the community is changing demographically, the school remains 98-percent Anglo, 100-percent upper-middle-class.

The vote last month was 7 to 5 to establish the diversity fund and has caused a stir among the teachers, staff, and parents.

"Let's try to bring closure to the scholarship-fund debate," Marsha states. "It seems to have caused quite a fuss and I don't know why."

"I'll tell you why," Maria responds. "It's because this place is filled with racists and yuppies. Only in a backward place like Cincinnati would people not want diversity!"

"Whoa, hold on. Why do we need diversity?" asks Phil, elder [*Antagonist #1*] statesman of the board. Phil's family was part of the first 20 families that enrolled students in the school when it opened in 1970. He is also the school's largest donor.

"This is the United States of America!" he continues. "I didn't want the diversity fund because those people are loafers. It's bad enough my tax dollars are going to them. I definitely don't want my school donations contributing to their sin.

"Look, Marsha, if I had known you wanted those types of students in this school, we would have never hired you in the first place."

Marsha is dumbfounded by Phil's comment. Before she can respond, an equally exasperated Maria chimes back in.

"Sin? What have they done?" Maria asks. [*Proponent #1*]

"Well, for starters, the poor ones won't go to work," he fires back. "The Bible says if a man won't work he shouldn't eat. We all know they are on the government dole. I didn't come from money. My parents did what they had to do for the family to make it.

"We didn't get one red cent from welfare programs. Why can't they do the same? They've got to learn to pull themselves up by their own bootstraps. And why should race be tied into who gets financial help? We're Christians. I mean, when I see a black man all I see is a man. I don't see color." [*Proponent #2*]

"Grandpa, chillax!" Mike interrupts. "I mean, who even talks like that anymore?" Mike is an architect, the newest member of the board, and Phil's 25-year-old grandson.

"This fund is needed to give us both ethnic and economic diversity,"

23

he continues. "Have you looked at the neighborhood lately? Better yet, have you looked at the world? We are doing our students a disservice if we don't bring the real world into the building."

"Dr. Liou," Marsha interjects, to call a halt to the generational family feud. "Do you have an opinion? I really would like to hear your perspective."

"Research shows that most students and families of low income, if given the proper help, achieve at the same rate as students in other social classes," Dr. Liou replies. "So I voted for the fund to offer that help."

"Look," Phil adds, "I am just expressing good old-fashioned values. I'm not condemning them. I just expect more from them. This is America, where we can all make it.

"How can we be operating as Christians if we support a Democratic platform like diversity? Marsha and Maria, I know you are women and want to mother everybody, but you two are going too far. You've got to think like men on this; kids nowadays need tough love, not handouts."

"We're not talking about handouts with this fund, but a hand-up," Maria argues. "Phil, I'll tell you what: There were many, many times that if my family didn't get help from the government, I would not have eaten. Offering them help with their education is the least we can do.

"That's why I voted for it. You can't make it in this country without an education. Combine that with the gospel, and that's the best hand-up you can give somebody."

"Well, this school will be looking for a hand-up soon." Phil says. "Our best teacher has left and I'm sure others will follow. At the last parent meeting we almost had a mutiny on our hands. I've been told there are major donors who are going to demand we shut down the diversity fund or they will pull their money out, which is going to hurt us big-time financially. What are we going to do about this?"

Everyone's eyes immediately turn to Marsha.

****

Heath heads up the interstate to Hicksville to spend the day with his father, Chuck. His Dad has always been his biggest source of wisdom about not only ministry, but life in general. After exchanging pleasantries over lunch and hearing about the elder situation, Chuck offers some advice.

"Son, to tell you the truth, I don't know if you have a solvable problem."

"That can't be true, Dad. I mean, they make it work in the secular world. They deal with these types of issues all the time."

"It's different for them," Chuck replies. "They have laws they have to follow, and money is tied to integration and things like that. You run a church. In a church, people only do things if they want to. The only power you have is influence."

"Isn't the gospel supposed to solve all problems?" Matt asks. "In college they stuffed cross-cultural learning down our throat and stressed how people need to be united. And then during that six-month internship I did at a diverse urban church, I matured in my faith so rapidly. Why can't I make it work now?"

"That was the pie-in-the-sky world of college," Chuck reminds his son. "This is real life. And Don has a point: You and Marsha loved living downtown when you were first married, but when you were expecting your first child, you turned down the offer to become pastor of an urban church because of the same issues Don raised."

Matt feels his stomach churn as his dad continues.

"You've read the same church-growth books I have. They basically tell you that mixing cultures is like mixing oil and water. Your ministry was doing fine until this open-gym controversy came up. I don't know what to tell you, because I don't have to deal with that type of stuff out here."

"Not yet," Heath answers. "There's that group of businessmen who want to bring in the meat-packing plant. Latino families will come here in droves if that happens."

"Look, Heath, it's just different out here." They're both silent for a few long moments. Then Chuck speaks up: "You know, now that I think about it, I may have an answer to your problem."

"I'm listening," Heath replies.

"Well, I told my elder board two weeks ago that I'll be ready to retire soon. Thirty years in the ministry is long enough. The first thing they asked was, would Heath be willing to come home to take over? I told them no, but that was before I knew about this situation. Heath, it's only going to get worse concerning this diversity stuff. Maybe you ought to come back to Hicksville."

"What about Marsha? She loves her job."

"Well, you know that the high school principal is a member of my church. I overheard him say the other day he will be looking for a new assistant principal. I could investigate if you want."

"I don't know what I want, Dad. I just don't know."

****

As she drives home from the board meeting, Marsha has the biggest headache ever. Both sides seem to have good points. Maria is right: Christians are supposed to help the poor.

But she knows that Phil is right too: Mr. Phelps' leaving was a major blow, and if some major donors leave it will cause financial hardship.

This also has the potential to create a major perception problem in the community. Marsha is leaning toward being practical about the whole matter. She could take the proposal off the table and reason that the school isn't ready for a move like this.

That would make the whole thing go away for the most part, and she would just have to smooth things over with a couple of board members.

But she can't convince herself that this is the biblical thing to do. After all, the majority of the board feels that the time is right, regardless of the consequences.

Marsha also feels guilty. She drove her parents crazy because she refused to go to Christian, rural Cedarville University herself as a student. With missionary zeal she went to the University of Cincinnati in order to take her faith to the "real world."

She remembers all of the diverse friendships she made while there, and the time she led her Muslim roommate to the Lord. She remembers the volunteering she did in the poorer areas of Cincinnati through the Christian campus group.

She also remembers how she and Heath bought an old, rundown duplex early in their marriage and rehabbed it to help change the community.

But everything changed when she became pregnant. When Heath had to choose between pastorates, they chose the one in North College Hill, because they felt that would be the most comfortable family life.

Before pregnancy she was gung-ho about tackling diversity, but when push came to shove she wanted to be comfortable. Now, she feels privileged and guilty that she even had the choice to lead a more comfortable life.

In fact, this controversy has made her realize that guilt was what drove her to embrace diversity in the first place; the guilt she felt for growing up white and upper-middle-class in a society that she feels favors her. She believes that people of color and of low income are treated unjustly in this country and she wants to make restitution.

But why should I feel guilty? she thinks. She doesn't use any racial slurs and she supports immigration reform. She's respectful to people of other ethnicities and social classes and will raise her children to be as well. Maybe she should just realize that she can't save the world but she can save the school.

The more she thinks, the worse her headache becomes.

Chapter Two
Reuniting the Family

Why do the nations rage and the people plot in vain?
Psalm 2:1

When I consult with Christian leaders about reconciliation, the conversation typically arises because something has happened on the grassroots level of their lives or ministry in the area of race relations. Perhaps the neighborhood around the ministry has changed or the leader's daughter has married someone of a different race.

Upon investigation, I often find that while Christian leaders are familiar with racial reconciliation they know little about *biblical* reconciliation. Practically speaking, two vitally important things must happen concerning the art of doing reconciliation: defining reconciliation in a post-racial world and establishing the biblical foundation for practicing it.

The term *reconciliation* has officially reached "buzzword" status — those words we frequently throw around but of which we rarely know the true meaning. A huge chunk of my time is spent simply defining the term scripturally. Over the years I have figured out that when I say *reconciliation*, people hear:

- peacemaking
- social gospel
- social justice
- blacks and whites getting along
- cultural diversity
- universalism
- liberalism
- Democratic party supporter
- political correctness

Because of the multiple meanings out there, we can't carry on a clear conversation. And so we tend to stay on the surface of this crucial topic — unaware of assumptions we are making. I believe that this lack of serious consideration truly hampers our personal spiritual growth.

Two significant assumptions underlie conversations about reconciliation in the Christian world today. Both ultimately hinder rather than help reconciliation efforts, and unless we reshape the way we think and act, we will not take significant steps forward in a globalized world.

The first assumption is that reconciliation is a nice idea, but not necessary. Yes, God loves all people and we should too. Yet we don't think we are all that bad or that the divisions are all that deep. And we're wary of walking into a neo-liberal social gospel, where any kind of lifestyle is acceptable as long as we all get along. So while we like the biblical concept of reconciliation, we believe that pursuing reconciliation beyond our current efforts is not necessary and may even be seen as theologically dangerous.

The second assumption in the conversation is that when we use the term *reconciliation*, we are focusing only on race and, more specifically, on black/white relations. The discussion does not reflect our transitioning, post-racial society or, more importantly, the biblical context in which reconciliation is framed.

We need to engage in a renewed conversation about reconciliation — redefine our terms and fully grasp why it matters so much. A rehash of the old muddled conversation just won't do.

The situation is similar to a recent visit I had with my doctor. Throughout my life, until my mid-20s, I was active in athletics. I could eat anything I wanted and it didn't matter. I actually had a hard time gaining weight.

As my life became more sedentary, my eating habits did not change and my weight began to reflect that fact. Like most people, I knew something ought to change, but a few extra pounds were not sufficient motivation. After all, I wasn't obese. I was just carrying a bit more baggage than in my youth.

Then last year my doctor gave me a whole new perspective. He told me that if I did not shed some weight, I was on a fast track to diabetes. That was what I would call a renewed conversation, i.e. renewal had taken place in my worldview concerning the effect on my life that weight gain caused.

Rather than remaining stuck in my previous, comfortable way of thinking, I chose to look at my habits in a whole new light. If I did not change, there was danger ahead. That conversation led to action, and over the following months I changed the way I ate and I now exercise regularly.

I have lost weight and made great progress toward avoiding diabetes. But I will never be able to say that I have arrived at a place where the work is done and I can go back to my old way of living, because my health is at stake. I must live differently until the Lord decides to take me home.

Now let me play the role of "doctor" and draw several parallels concerning the body of Christ and reconciliation. First, most people have a sense that something ought to change in their personal faith and ministry concerning reconciliation, but even though they may be carrying some "extra weight," they really don't think things are that bad.

However, I propose that if we don't start to live differently, not only will our ministries not be of optimum health, but eventually we will also lose a measure of evangelistic effectiveness due to demographic changes.

Second, no matter how much progress we make, the work will never be done. Successful reconciliation requires a lifestyle change. My doctor had warned me about fad diets, which are short-term gain, long-term pain. The reconciliation "fad diets" of one-time events, pulpit exchanges, and apologies will not get it done. Reconciliation conversation must lead to long-term action.

Third, primary motivation to change will require a new perspective. That perspective must be rooted in the Scriptures, not peace studies, social analysis, or good intentions. Such things are helpful, but our path for life change is deep theological reflection followed by practical social action.

There is a direct correlation between spiritual maturity and the ability to lead with reconciliation in mind. I have yet to meet a person who has been successful in practicing reconciliation who isn't also mature in his or her faith.

The journey of reconciliation begins within. You can't lead anybody anywhere that you haven't been yourself. Reconciliation cannot be faked. It is not a trendy new technique to be more in tune with the culture. It is an expression of God's work within you.

Three years into the planting of River of Life church, things were going extremely well. We started with my family and had grown to around 100 people. Through the wonderful generosity of our parent church, we had obtained an old hardware store of 33,000 square feet to renovate. Through the gifts of foundations and Christian business professionals, $350,000 had been raised toward renovation. We were on our way. Or so I thought.

In a six-month period we lost 35 people, all of them white. I began to do exit interviews and could not believe my ears as to the reasons people left. I am very aware that many churches experience a mass exodus for various reasons, but the reasons I heard were ominous: "We don't believe the races should worship together; I don't want my kids involved with poor kids; black people are too loud; your wife shouldn't be on stage opening up the service because a man should do it."

Those exit interviews pretty much destroyed me. I was discouraged. Here were people in whom I had invested for three years, and they basically bailed on me and the vision. To be honest, my spirit was weak, my will failing, and I was ready to resign. But before I did, I decided to go on a three-day fast and seek wisdom. After I emerged, it was clear that God was not calling me to quit. He was calling me to transform my practice of reconciliation from a social to a biblical foundation.

Biblical Foundation: Family Feud

So let's do some brief theological reflection, beginning with the real-world perspective of the biblical story. The Bible is a collection of stories whose intent is to reframe the world (reality) through the lens of God. Readers are then challenged to submit to the reality presented in Scripture, love the God who is represented, and live out His commands.

To understand reconciliation from a biblical point of view, we must see how it operates throughout Scripture — from the very beginning (Genesis), through the ebb and flow of sin and division, to the end. We must see how reconciliation is *God's* idea.

For starters, we can think of the people of the world as one giant family — large, colorful, diverse . . . and dysfunctional! The Bible then depicts a world of smaller, competing families, known as nations. The links that form these families are ethnic cultural groups, whose members share familiar origins and basics of culture such language, values, attitudes, and beliefs.

Throughout history, as recorded in textbooks as well as in the Old Testament, we see a theme of struggle, discrimination, and conflict: one story after another of individuals and cultural groups trying to advance their own interests over others. It is a sure recipe for division rather than unity.

If we are not careful, as we follow the biblical story we might mistakenly think that other people are "the enemy" — other people being non-believers in God. Yet in reality, we face a powerful spiritual army of evil beings whose goal is to frustrate God's efforts toward a united, inclusive family:

For our struggle is not against flesh and blood, but against the rulers, against the authorities, against the powers of this dark world and against the spiritual forces of evil in the heavenly realms. (Eph. 6:12)

When we watch the news and see stories of "ethnic cleansing," or of women being sold as sex slaves; or when we look at a history book and see that once upon a time the U.S. government allowed the enslavement of a group of people based on their African heritage, we cannot forget that the root of these events is spiritual. Therefore the primary way to address these and other evil atrocities should be rooted in spiritual practice as well.

When it comes to reconciliation, the first step of the church in a deeply broken world is not strategy, but prayer. Joseph Cardinal Bernardin wrote in *The Gift of Peace* that prayer was "closing the gap between what I am and what God wants of me." We will not be successful unless we develop a vibrant, strong prayer life to close the gap.

The gap exists because as sinners we are all in some degree of rebellion against God. Psalms 2:1 asks, "Why do the nations conspire and the peoples plot in vain?" The quick answer is because they are in rebellion. Let's now take a look at the root of the rebellion.

In Genesis 2 we see God's plan for unity in the Garden of Eden. Relationships were perfect between people and God, between people themselves, and with the environment. It was truly a blessed state of existence.

Actually, the word *blessed* does not accurately describe what was going on. A better word is a Hebrew one, *shalom. Shalom* means people living in a situation of completeness in every aspect of their human existence.

Take a moment and do this little exercise. Write down every single need that you have in your life. Don't leave any out. Now write down every single need you can think of that the world has. After compiling your list, imagine if they all disappeared forever. That's *shalom.*

In the Garden of Eden, Adam and Eve experienced *shalom.* Their physical, social, moral, mental, and emotional needs were completely met. And their spiritual relationship with God was without filters — 100-percent pure. Theirs was a life with no worries.

Then, the familiar story of Genesis 3 tells of the moment when the whole situation of *shalom* unraveled, beginning the dysfunctional mess of a family we have today. By "mess" I mean the change that occurs in the personal character of humans, brought about by the willful disobedience of Adam and Eve. With their sin, God's original intent for our world — to live in unity with each other and with Him — was violated.

The consequences of the Fall are instant: Confidence is replaced by doubt. Honesty is replaced by deception. Intimacy is replaced by shame. Fellowship is replaced by fear.

In essence, we see barriers go up between Adam and Eve and between both them and God. And along with the barriers come hostility. God questions Adam, Adam blames Eve, and Eve blames the snake. Adam and Eve show here the first signs of human conflict and rebellion against God, a rebellion that continues to have far-reaching effects. In Genesis 3:15, God speaks to the evil being (represented by the serpent) who started it all:

> And I will put enmity between you and the woman, and between your offspring and hers; he will crush your head, and you will strike his heel.

This verse foretells how our world will be in continual conflict between humans and representatives of evil. The battle lines have been formed, and the world from now until Christ's return will struggle in a messy conflict. The apostle Paul calls the time between the Fall and Christ's return "this present evil age" (Galatians 1:4).

Traditionally, Genesis 3:15 is also interpreted as a foreshadowing of Christ's eventual defeat of Satan. We know that Christ came to reconcile people to their God, to each other, and to creation.

Let's now reflect on how Christ entered the world. A good place to start is Abraham and Sarah. In Genesis 12:2-3 God promises them:

> I will make you into a great nation and I will bless you; I will make your name great, and you will be a blessing. I will bless those who bless you, and whoever curses you I will curse; and all peoples on earth will be blessed through you.

See once again God's desire for unity: a unified nation, bringing blessing to all. Yet to receive the promise of God, Abraham must make a few choices: Stay in this familiar land, or go to a new one? Stay with his biological family and promised inheritance, or leave to start a new family with his (infertile) wife?

All the choices boil down to whether Abraham is going to trust God and obey the call on his life. He must act in faith. Abraham left behind more than family and comfort when he chose to follow God; he also left behind cultural tradition. Let me explain.

In the ancient world, it was thought that gods were bound by certain criteria — one of which was that a god could not cross national borders. The god of Ur and the Chaldeans could not be the god of, say, Egypt and the Egyptians. In other words, gods were segregated by ethnic enclaves.

The God of the Hebrews was challenging Abraham to break out of that belief system, declaring that He was the type of God who could travel anywhere and be over any people group. By agreeing to move, Abraham was agreeing to convert to an entirely different religious tradition. He truly was exhibiting tremendous faith.

In Genesis 15, God brings even more clarity to His plan for using Abraham and Sarah to restore unity. He declares that they will have a son, and their offspring will fulfill the promise of blessing all the people of the world.

In Genesis 26:4, God reminds Abraham's son Isaac of that promise. Then, in Genesis 28:4, He reminds Isaac's son Jacob of the promise as well. The very existence of a genealogy is in itself a confirmation of the promise.

The tangible blessing does not come overnight. After Genesis, the story expands beyond individuals to the complete sum of Abraham's offspring, which eventually become known as the nation of Israel. In Exodus we see the pitting of nation against nation as a contest between gods.

For example, the famous plagues of Exodus 1-12 were each a contest between the God of Israel and one of Egypt's gods. When God rescued the Israelites, He delivered the message that the God of Israel is the sovereign God over all, regardless of your cultural family. As more and more non-Israelites recognized this, they switched allegiances.

Consider Joshua 2 and the story of Rahab; read the story of Naomi and Ruth in the Book of Ruth; ponder God's message to the Israelite captives in Babylon found in Jeremiah 29:4-7. Throughout the Old Testament the message to the Israelites was clear: *Through your lives you will declare the glory of the one true God to those who don't know Me; and through this declaration, they will come to Me.*

Biblical Foundation: Family Reunion

We see from this brief look at the Old Testament that the main way to a relationship with God was to have a relationship with His people — Abraham's biological descendents, the nation of Israel. People who wanted to know God needed to come through them.

In the New Testament this is no longer the case. The apostle Paul makes this clear when he reminds the Galatians that they began their relationship with God the same way Abraham did: by faith (Galatians 3:6-9). Abraham's real offspring are those who have faith in his God. The redemption of Christ permits *all* to enjoy the blessing of Abraham (Galatians 3:14).

If people want to know God, they need not seek out Israelites and convert to Judaism. That was the old paradigm. We are now told to receive the promise of the Spirit and form communities of Spirit-filled people. These ministry communities are the primary vehicles for the nations to know God.

The stress of the New Testament is toward a community of people making their presence known by living differently as the people of God in their geographic region. As they do this, the people of their region will know where to look for God. For example, take a look at Ephesians 5:1-16:

Be imitators of God, therefore, as dearly loved children and live a life of love, just as Christ loved us and gave himself up for us as a fragrant offering and sacrifice to God. But among you there must not be even a hint of sexual immorality, or of any kind of impurity, or of greed, because these are improper for God's holy people. Nor should there be obscenity, foolish talk or coarse joking, which are out of place, but rather thanksgiving ... Be very careful, then, how you live—not as unwise but as wise, making the most of every opportunity, because the days are evil.

You can find an example of these ethical encouragements in all of Paul's writings to churches. These instructions of how to live the Christian life are not geared toward individuals, but rather toward the community of believers. The concern is with the character of the church, stressing how the people of God should live in a rebellious, conflicted world.

This is no small concern, as nothing less than the essence of the gospel is at stake. Jesus set a clear pattern concerning how the gospel was going to spread: people influencing others to follow Jesus through the witness of their lives.

First there were 12 (John 1:35-50); then 72 (Luke 10:1); then at least 120 (Acts 1:15); then more than 3,000 (Acts 2:41); then millions, all through the simple concept of Spirit-filled communities living differently from the world around them. We are citizens of the Kingdom of God, a holy nation that acts as ambassadors of reconciliation to a conflicted world in rebellion (2 Corinthians 5:11-21).

In a reunited family, value and significance don't lie in race, ethnicity, power, wealth, gender, or any other attitude found in the rebellious world. In the reunited family called the Church, our values, attitudes, and beliefs have been radically restructured through the power of the Holy Spirit (Galatians 3:26-29). The source of this reunited family is none other than God.

We are told in 2 Corinthians 5:18 that God gave the church the *gift* of reconciliation. In a world where conflict reigns supreme, only God can cause a family reunion of all people. It is God's initiative and God's work. The reunited family called the Church then becomes a witness to a world marred by conflict.

Reflection:

Did you learn anything new? Write a summary.

Action:

Share what you have learned with someone. You might . . .

- preach a sermon based on this chapter;
- teach this chapter as a devotional or small-group lesson;
- take a friend or two out to dinner and discuss what you have learned;
- blog or post a Facebook note and invite your friends to comment.

Chapter Three
Renewing the Reconciliation Conversation

Do not conform any longer to the pattern of this world, but be transformed by the renewing of your mind . . .

Romans 12:2

Now that we have biblically defined reconciliation, let's talk about the endgame. As leaders, our overarching goal is to build ministry communities that have the ability to reverse the divisions of humanity and multiply kingdom growth. We want to live differently in order to become a witness to a rebellious world. I say to you and your community, *A Cruce Salus.*

Do you know what the phrase means? You will have to wait a few pages before I tell you. It illustrates a point I am making in this chapter.

A huge blind spot in our efforts of practicing reconciliation is that of not realizing we need common ground to communicate with each other. Operating on common ground is crucial, because we are in what scholars are labeling the post-racial era. What *post-racial* means depends on which expert you ask, so I won't provide a definition. For our purposes, what we need to understand is that things are changing rapidly concerning racial identity.

Our Post-Racial Era

Let's take a brief moment to think about race. Racial identity is based on physical, or biological, characteristics such as skin color. The *social* perception is that these physical characteristics make us vastly different from one another. Ironically, scientists have proven over and over again that there is no biological difference of significance between people.

If I need a blood transfusion, what matters most is my blood type, not my racial category. In fact, biologically speaking there is just the human race. If this is the case, you might be wondering why race is so prevalent in our thought if it is not based in biological science.

To be honest, that's another book in itself. But for our purposes, you'll just have to trust me or check me out on my facts by doing some personal research of your own.

Just because race doesn't exist biologically doesn't mean it doesn't exist. Race is what is called a *social construction*, meaning that people believe it exists and thus live their lives accordingly. So although race is not based in biology, we still have to deal with it because it is a sociological reality. What has changed in our society is how we deal with race. This chart summarizes the evolution of racial identity in America:

Time Period	Racial Era	Worldview
Before 1950	Segregation	Non-white is "less than."
1950s	Desegregation	Non-white is disadvantaged.
1960s	Integration	Non-white is missing.
1970s	Multiculturalism	More identities than race emerge in public discourse.
1980s	Cultural Diversity	Racial identity is "watered down."
1990s	Cultural Competence	Race is one of many identity categories
21st century	Globalization	Post-racial

Prior to 1950, the norm was segregation. Once our groundbreaking civil rights legislation took effect, integration and equal rights really began to take root.

During the '60s, women's issues joined the race-based civil rights movement. The force behind change during both the '50s and '60s was legal in nature. With legal victories, a new paradigm then began to take shape in the 1970s: multiculturalism.

This was a significant worldview transition. Prior to the '70s, the spotlight had been on assimilation into an American "melting pot" — a metaphor for all cultures melting into mainstream culture. Mainstream culture usually meant white, Protestant, male, heterosexual, and middle class.

With the emergence of multiculturalism, people questioned the appropriateness of the melting pot. Multiculturalism can be thought of as a "salad." As in a salad, each culture keeps its distinctive characteristics. The tomato remains a tomato, lettuce remains lettuce, and croutons remain croutons. No one culture is asked to melt into another.

The new metaphor of a salad began to prevail, and by the 1980s, cultural diversity began to be the new norm. Corporate America discovered that it was good business to address and market based on race, ethnicity, and gender, as well as other distinct cultural categories such as sexuality. Many companies implemented cultural-diversity training in earnest for their employees and developed marketing strategies to target different cultural groups.

By the 1990s cultural competence was becoming the new norm. Cultural competency is the art and science of intentional interaction with other cultural groups. From a Christian perspective, it is not a coincidence that predominately white Christian groups such as Promise Keepers began to focus on the topic of reconciliation. They and many others obviously sensed the signs of the times.

Like the shift to multiculutralism in the '70s, we are now in the midst of a transitional shift: globalization. Globalization is a catch-all phrase that describes how social institutions of the world (political, economic, family, religious, and educational) are moving toward forming global citizens. The challenge is to function together in that capacity.

Thomas L. Friedman in his book *The World Is Flat* proposes that the pace of globalization is quickening and will continue to have a growing impact on how institutions function. As ministry leaders we must pay attention to this shift.

One of the places where I recently led a workshop on this topic, with great response, was in Wichita, Kansas. There I addressed hundreds of church leaders who were from mainly Nebraska, Kansas, and Missouri. When I would ask a leader where he or she was from, the opening comment always seemed to be, "Well, it's in the middle of nowhere, but I'm from..."

Why on earth would church leaders from the middle of nowhere — states not known for ethnic diversity — want to hear about reconciliation? Well, a common thread was how their towns were being flooded by people from all over the world, mainly due to the decisions of global corporations.

I know a pastor in Florence, Kentucky who translates his worship service from English to Japanese. Why? Toyota has its North American manufacturing headquarters nearby and they are taking advantage of the opportunity to bring the gospel to the executive management that works there. That's a prime example of how globalization should affect our ministry practice.

God is in the middle of bringing the world to our doorstep. Is your ministry ready to reap the harvest?

In addition to globalization, we are dealing with *cross-generational worldviews*. There are four generational groups often found in our ministries:

- Builders (born before and up to 1945)
- Boomers (1946-1964)
- Busters, or Gen X (1965-1983)
- Bridgers, or Millennials (1984 and later)

If you look back at the racial era chart, you can see that we are dealing with segregation, desegregation, integration, multiculturalism, cultural diversity, cultural competence, and globalization mindsets all at once. The word *race* is loaded with meaning, typically based on generational worldview.

Which brings me to another point: In a globalized world, the trend is that people are choosing to *not* primarily identify themselves by race. Ethnic, gender and sexual preference are just a few examples that are common as primary identification in the 21st century.

One time I was presenting a workshop on reconciliation using globalized language (I'll talk more about how to do that later). Afterward, an African-American whom I'll call Jerome came up to talk to me. He was so grateful for my presentation.

He worked for a Christian organization that had hired him in the name of reconciliation and expected him to bring the racial perspective of the *entire* black community into their ministry. Besides the inability of anyone to do that, his main problem was that he didn't limit his identity strictly to race. In fact, it wasn't even his primary identity.

He knew he was black, but he had grown up in an extremely multiethnic context where people identified themselves through cultural, not racial, characteristics (neighborhood, language spoken, economic class, musical tastes, etc.). So he had no knowledge of the race-based "black experience" his organization expected him to bring. His dilemma was that he was a black man without the traditional black experience! He struggled with what to do about the situation.

Let me be honest. Most of both my black and white colleagues are just flat-out tired of talking about "racial" reconciliation. Or, to be more accurate, I should say that they are tired of conversations in schizo-phrenic, emotionally-charged language based in historical distrust that doesn't reflect our globalized historical moment.

I am sure many of you have participated in these kinds of conversa-tions. You know, the ones with the mythological premise that all white people (particularly males) are evil, rich, and guilty; all black people are moral, poor, and just dying to have a white friend. And if you aren't black or white, there is no room for you or your ideas and concerns.

My Latino, Asian, and Native American colleagues are ready for a renewed conversation. They have frequently told me stories of being excluded from the reconciliation mix. For instance, how are we going to talk about immigration (which should be part of the reconciliation con-versation) if things are constantly being framed in black vs. white racial language? There also isn't room to engage other barriers that keep us di-vided. No room for gender, age, social class, special needs, or anything else that doesn't fit into the black/white racial paradigm.

Before I move on, let me quickly address a conclusion that you may be wrongly jumping to. I am not saying we should ignore racial issues. Race still matters. Although we are moving toward a post-racial society (however it is defined), we are nowhere near arriving there. In fact, I have serious doubts we will ever get there (at least totally) in my lifetime. So of course it should be part of the conversation.

What I am saying is it should not be *the only* conversation. If race comes up, great; go ahead and deal with it, but in an inclusive way so that all racial and ethnic groups can participate. When we limit recon-ciliation to black/white racial dynamics, it is like using a dead language (like Latin).

At one time Latin was relevant, but today most people don't have a clue how to speak it. At the beginning of this chapter I used the phrase

A Cruce Salus, which in Latin means "from the cross comes salvation." I would guess that most of you didn't know the phrase. Yet you would agree that it is a phrase with meaning well worth knowing. Similarly, if we don't change the language of reconciliation conversations, they are increasingly going to sound like Latin to a globalized world. I have found many people who want to participate. Ironically, they are excluded from the conversation by the myopic black/white hyper focus.

Do you want people in your ministry community to engage with you in this? Drop the old racial mindset of black vs. white from your reconciliation conversation and start talking about reconciling people to God and to each other – period. The fact is, the Bible never asks us to focus *exclusively* on race when it comes to reconciliation. When addressing reconciliation, Scripture speaks of holistic reconciliation, meaning overcoming *all* barriers that divide, as we read in the section "Biblical Foundation: Family Reunion."

Using Globalized Language

Previously, I introduced you to Jerome, my African-American friend who was searching for a way to talk more holistically about reconciliation within his predominately white ministry community. Let me introduce you to two more colleagues who are wrestling with how to lead with reconciliation in mind in a globalized world.

I'll start with Tammy. She is an Asian, 30-something Christian who left her corporate job to work for an inner-city ministry. Everything about her life communicates that she "gets it" concerning reconciliation.

A couple of weeks into our friendship, she came into my office, visibly upset and looking for guidance. Why? She had experienced major friction with some of the people of color on her ministry staff. She's also frequently disrespected by the staff because she is female.

Another issue she expressed was that none of the poor people who utilized the services of the ministry were eager to relate with her. She had changed the course of her life to become a reconciler, and she lamented the fact that although she had great intentions concerning reconciliation, she was failing miserably.

Another friend is Allen, who grew up in the Midwest as the son of a pastor. While the civil rights movement had changed things in some places, the full ripples had not quite reached where he was living. His world exploded, however, when his family moved to southern California the summer before high school. Suddenly, he was surrounded by more languages and skin tones then he could have imagined. As a white male in the minority, he learned quickly to adapt.

Today, Allen pastors a 99-percent white, suburban, upper-middle-class church. But the neighborhood around him is filled with ethnic diversity. He desires to effectively minister to his neighbors, as well as to the poor who live in other parts of his city.

Tammy, Allen, and Jerome are part of a growing trend of globalized ministers. If you are reading this book, you are probably part of that trend. How can we lead our ministry communities into a more effective place of ministry in a time such as this?

Consider this analogy. Occasionally I receive free tickets to a sporting event. Sometimes I get cheap seats in the upper deck, from where the participants look like ants; more often I get tickets to great seats. When you sit in great seats, the action is so vivid and intense, the amenities so great, you literally feel that you are part of the game.

What if I gave you those tickets? And what if after the game, you did a little experiment? You asked ten different people sitting in totally different parts of the stadium, "What happened?" You know what you would get? Ten answers containing both similarities and differences.

In fact, although everybody was watching the same game in the same stadium, you might not be able to tell that based on the variety of responses. How you view the game is *totally* dependent on your seat location. People in the great seats would have a different perspective from those who sit in the cheap seats, even though they saw the same game in the same stadium.

Now imagine that you have tickets to the game of life. If you think of life as a game being played in a stadium, then *culture* is the seat and stadium from which you view the game. Everyone in the stadium can see the action, but no one sees it exactly the same. They have only the perspective of their seat location. That is the practical implication culture has on us.

To describe this tension among Christians, historian Andrew Walls uses the term the twin forces of Christian history, describing an *indigenizing* principle and a *pilgrim* principle.

The *indigenizing principle* ensures that there is no such thing as a Christian who is not influenced heavily by the culture to which he or she belongs. In fact, the indigenizing principle points out that the gospel must make sense culturally in order for us to accept Christ. Because culture provides the framework for understanding and living the Christian life, it is easy to steer Christian beliefs toward particular cultural interests and think we are doing nothing wrong.

Because we are somewhat a prisoner to our culture, we need to be liberated from some aspects of it. Walls describes this liberating force as the *pilgrim principle*. The indigenizing principle accepts the culture that a person possesses. Paradoxically, the pilgrim principle requires that Christians *change* some of the culture to which they are bound, to match up with biblical teachings.

We can make our personal lives and ministries so culturally comfortable that only people who are just like us can have a place at the table. This fact makes it critical to constantly examine the tension of the twin forces.

We must look at our lives and ministries through culture in order to speak a common language that matches the globalized world in which we live.

I like to think of our identity as a pie. Each slice is a representation of the whole of who we are. Here are few slices of the cultural pie that I think hold particular relevance in our society:

• *Race* — physical distinctions present at birth, to which cultural importance has been assigned
• *Ethnicity* — people who share history, cultural roots, and a sense of identity
• *Social class* — people who share similar economic and cultural status
• *Age* — period of life
• *Gender* — expected behaviors based on biological sex

Culturally speaking, here are a few descriptors of me: racially black, ethnically of African descent, white-collar social class, 39 years of age, and biologically male. In addition, I live in Cincinnati, Ohio; and I am a military veteran, a husband, and a Christian. I could go on for pages describing the slices of my cultural pie.

Each one of the descriptors that I used has played a role in forming who I am. Overall, I may be part of the American culture. But I am also part of the Midwestern, northern, urban, male, African-American, Christian cultures. If you change any one of those factors, it affects my identity.

Sociologists often use the illustration of a toolkit to help us understand the role of culture in our lives. Culture gives us the tools that we need to deal with the problems of everyday life. These tools shape how we view our world. One tool is *values*. Think of values as ideas that are commonly shared, or goals that are desired by group members.

When we talk about values, we are talking about whether something is right or wrong. Although there are many value differences between cultural groups, there do seem to be some that are universal. For instance, every culture seems to value the concept of families, although cultural groups differ in how they define the necessities of a "good" family.

Values help us determine what we consider to be *normal*. Every cultural group has rules of behavior — often learned innately rather than taught — and if someone violates those rules, they are considered abnormal. The rules provide our plan for living.

For instance, as someone with two graduate degrees who regularly teaches in formal settings, I am expected to behave a certain way. My usual dress is dress slacks and a dress shirt. My language is Standard English.

If I walked into one of the settings where I normally teach wearing oversized, baggy jeans with no belt, a baseball hat on backward and an oversized white T-shirt, and I spoke Hip Hop slang, it would be safe to say that most would be shocked by my appearance and behavior. Why? It would not fit the cultural norm.

So let me now land the cultural airplane, so to speak. The racial division reflected within our society is a symptom of a much larger issue: not understanding the role of culture in our lives. And it holds true in the Christian community as well. The genius of talking about reconciliation using cultural language is that now there is a language for *everyone* to bring their topics to the table.

Go ahead and talk about race. But let's not pretend that race is the main thing on people's minds in a globalized culture. There are social class and generational dynamics that need to be discussed in the same breath.

And now that we are talking about things culturally, there is plenty of room for the immigration dialogue and the invisibility of Asian and Native American ministry concerns. If there are any women's or generational issues within your ministry community, we can put those onto the reconciliation table, too, in a way that is understood by all. Basically, when using the language of culture, the reconciliation conversation subtly shifts from race-only to general in-out group dynamics.

By *in-group* I mean a group to which we feel an allegiance, or with whom we feel most comfortable. By *out-group* I mean a group that we find challenging to understand. We often see this group as the enemy. During my Ph.D. studies I was introduced to something called *Cultural Proficiency* by Dr. Ray Terrell:

Worldview	Focus
Cultural Destructiveness	The elimination of other people's cultures
Cultural Incapacity	Belief in the superiority of one's own culture and behavior that dis-empowers another's culture
Cultural Blindness	Acting as if the cultural differences one sees do not matter or not recognizing that there are differences among and between cultures
Cultural Pre-Competence	Awareness of the limitations of one's skills or an organization's practices when interacting with other cultural groups
Cultural Competence	Effective interaction with other cultural groups
Cultural Proficiency	Diverse cultures organically thrive within your organization

Destructiveness, incapacity, and blindness often lead to division and to following the world's pattern of conflict. I believe that Christian ministries are called, at the very least, to practice pre-competence and should strive for competence and proficiency. Speaking the language of culture is the way we start reversing division and multiplying kingdom growth.

What exactly makes up this language of culture? Essentially, it involves speaking in ways where we can understand our differences and act on our commonalities. Speaking the language of culture will give your ministry community a more holistic picture of reconciliation. By doing so, you will start creating a roadmap to operate in a globalized world. Here are several tips to successfully speak the language of culture:

Tip #1: Accept that culture is a powerful force that shapes our Christian values, attitudes, beliefs, and behaviors. Many times during presentations, somebody challenges me as to why we are even having the cultural discussion. They do not see the relevance of talking about race, ethnicity, social class, gender, etc., because the Bible says we are all one in Christ, the old has passed away and so forth. They believe that the Christian way is cultural blindness.

Yet our differences, in practical life, have not passed away. They affect us every day, so we need to acknowledge, assess, and place a value on these differences. For example, one time I attended a ministry retreat. During this time, each ministry leader took several minutes to talk about the highlights for the upcoming year.

One leader told jokes about and spoke in a denigrating way about women. Some people (both male and female) were understandably upset. This blatant devaluing of the talents of women should not have happened, especially within a Christian retreat setting. How would you address an incident like this?

Ministries that accept culture as a normal part of the human experience will acknowledge and appreciate differences instead of denigrating them. They will recognize that we view life from different seats in the stadium and that our differing perspective is valuable.

Tip #2: For successful reconciliation, cultural adaptation must happen. Have you ever heard someone say that everybody should be treated the same without any "special" treatment? This may sound good, but it is not reality. We actually must consider culture all the time in order to be successful.

One time a Christian ministry claimed to want to reach a first-generation Latino community, yet leadership had planned to cancel the Spanish broadcasts on its radio station. The broadcasts were considered "special" treatment of Latinos.

I don't know how you reach an entire people group and yet don't plan to speak their primary language! They changed their plans once their Latino constituents found out and expressed their displeasure.

What this ministry initially forgot to do is embrace the principle that culture shapes our lives and then make the adaptations necessary to further the kingdom. This is the most practical step that a ministry needs to take in order to practice reconciliation.

Cultural adaptation is not a foreign concept to ministries. Youth pastors regularly adapt Christian values, attitudes, and beliefs to cultural norms that youth understand. Capital-campaign consultants are hired to help church leadership communicate in cultural norms appreciated by people with financial resources to give.

For some reason, when it comes to certain cultural traits (particularly race, social class, and gender), we typically do not follow the same principle. Most differences based in cultural backgrounds are not inappropriate. Each culture elevates certain values, attitudes, and beliefs above others. Ministries should culturally adapt to connect these values to Scriptures and to the work of the Spirit.

Tip #3: Be aware of cultural differences while acting on shared values. As a Christian, if I were to draw a circle that represented my values and then you — as part of my community — were to draw a circle that represented your values, our circles would probably overlap significantly.

There would also be some values that we do not have in common, based on our culture. The question then becomes: Do we have so little in common that we cannot build a relationship with one another? My guess would be that, most of the time, the answer is no.

Reconcilers recognize that differences exist based on culture. They learn successful approaches for resolving conflict. They make reconciliation part of their DNA by obtaining cultural knowledge and applying it to their everyday living. They also provide spaces for significant communication to occur, to keep misunderstandings based on culture held to a minimum.

Reflection:

Describe your own cultural identity by rating each of the following on a scale of 1 to 10 (1 being not very important; 10 being extremely important). The numbers represent the importance of each of the following categories in your life. Be honest; this is not the time for political correctness. Everyone in your ministry community should share how they ranked themselves.

Cultural Category	Personal Importance
Age	
Biological sex	
Ethnic heritage (Irish, African, Mexican, Korean, etc.)	
Race (black, white, etc.)	
City, state, and neighborhood of residence	
Profession	
Religion	
Marital status	
Parental status	
Formal educational level	
Social class (white collar, blue collar, mix of both)	
Primary language	

Based on your answers, what makes up your in-group? How about your out-group? Again, honesty is required. We *all* have in- and out-groups in our lives.

Action:

Find three people from your out-group and treat them to a meal as a group or individually. Over the meal discuss your commonalities and differences. What insights did you gain?

Chapter Four
Reframing Your Ministry Community

So the word of God spread...

Acts 6:7

We've established our biblical foundation of reuniting the family, and we now understand that we must speak a language that reflects our globalized world. Next, let's talk about what happens within the community you lead as people regularly compare cultural notes. What I mean by comparing notes is to learn how our backgrounds affect our view of ministry. As we do this, we will be able to reframe ministry issues.

Carlito was an attendee at a conference where I made a presentation. He serves on a ministry staff in a western-state suburb of about 50,000 people. Most of the people are middle class or middle class "plus" in terms of income.

He describes his neighborhood as "bland, boring, and very crime-free, with lots of engineer types." The street he lives on represents the typical makeup of his community:

• House 1: White Jewish engineer married to a Latina court recorder with one teenage girl.

• House 2: Filipina divorced single mother executive assistant with two teenage boys.

• House 3: White retired airline operations manager married to a white "Cajun" woman from the South with no children.

• House 4: Filipino engineer married to a Filipina nurse, whom he met in Nigeria. Her grandmother lives with them and they have two elementary-age boys.

• House 5: White retired satellite engineer married to a white Norwegian, who are empty-nesters.

• House 6: Latino and Latina couple with no kids, who both have blue-collar jobs.

- House 7: White widower who is a retired banker.
- House 8: White widower who is a retired government employee.
- House 9: White male with a doctorate from Cambridge married to a Chinese woman. They have seven children ages 2 to 19.
- House 10: White retired Army colonel married to a white woman who is a VP for a non-profit organization.
- House 11: White home investor married to a Chinese nurse.

Maybe your block looks nothing like Carlito's, but demographers tell us that it won't be long before you see something similar. Even if you don't ever see it, you need to be aware, because it's the world the majority of us live in. The balance of the U.S. population lives in multiethnic, multi-class, mega-regions.

As you look at Carlito's street, if you were going to share Christ with his neighbors, where would you begin? Whatever you do, you need to be sure to reframe your ministry by managing the dynamics of difference.

In Romans 12:2 we are called to "not conform any longer to the pattern of this world." When it comes to diversity, those world patterns are usually selfish and demeaning. I find that is why so many Christians revolt against secular diversity initiatives: The world too often stops short of God's vision.

Typically, secular diversity is pursued as the end goal — an accomplishment and/or an experience to be had. This is not the case for believers. Reconciling people is about gaining Christ's point of view toward them, regardless of how different they are from us.

Just because the world may have a different vision concerning diversity is not a reason to not pursue diversity. In fact, we should desire to go deeper than they do. Healthy diversity is possible, but only when the Holy Spirit renews and redirects our minds toward transformation.

There is nothing biological that causes people to practice or not practice prejudice or discrimination. We learn it from our friends, family, media, and other life experiences. The key to transformation is to sort through our learning and decide what is Christ-like and what is not.

I learned in all my ministry stops that at the end of the day, we are all in the same boat. We are both saint and sinner. This lesson is foundational to how we view people.

We are constantly being pushed to believe that more money somehow makes us morally better. Or that one race or ethnicity of people is more inherently evil. Or that our gender, age or language makes us deserving of preferential treatment. Reconciliation forces us to move past both sympathy and supremacy. It makes us confront our "messiah complex" of thinking that we can save ourselves. It exposes our hearts and challenges our true beliefs about one another.

One of my favorite TV shows is "Flip This House." The show follows the lives of real estate developers in a number of cities. They buy homes, renovate them, and resell them for a profit. To gain Christ's perspective toward people, consider your life as a brick house. Each of the bricks represents an experience. Some experiences are good and some are awful. Nevertheless, they are yours. When Jesus comes in, He is the general contractor, creating something brand new. He desires to rehab you.

When it comes to reconciliation, some of us have had the gift of possessing many good bricks (experiences) used during our original construction. We've had many positive cross-cultural life experiences. Therefore we embrace reconciliation easily. Many of us, however, do not have these experiences and need to be rehabbed.

In fact, you might have had awful experiences cross-culturally. The bad news is that these experiences don't just go away. The good news of the gospel is that you can, if you so desire, work alongside the Holy Spirit in your rehabilitation efforts. You can also help rehab others.

I asked earlier how you might relate to Carlito's neighbors. Let's pretend that you figure that out and with great success. They are all now involved in your ministry. How are you going to *manage* your success?

A Model to Consider

I'm familiar with the story of a multi-ethnic, multi-cultural ministry community that experienced problems because of diversity. The church had cultural issues along the lines of ethnicity, gender, age, social class, and former religious backgrounds. You are probably familiar with this church as well, because its story can be found in Acts 6:1-7:

In those days when the number of disciples was increasing, the Grecian Jews among them complained against the Hebraic Jews because their widows were being overlooked in the daily distribution of food. So the Twelve gathered all the disciples together and said, "It would not be right for us to neglect the ministry of the word of God in order to wait on tables. Brothers, choose seven men from among you who are known to be full of the Spirit and wisdom. We will turn this responsibility over to them and will give our attention to prayer and the ministry of the word." This proposal pleased the whole group. They chose Stephen, a man full of faith and of the Holy Spirit; also Philip, Procorus, Nicanor, Timon, Parmenas, and Nicolas from Antioch, a convert to Judaism. They presented these men to the apostles, who prayed and laid their hands on them. So the word of God spread. The number of disciples in Jerusalem increased rapidly, and a large number of priests became obedient to the faith.

This passage of Scripture has played a special role in my life. It is a model of how to minister in a globalized world. As I mentioned earlier, in the third year of my church-planting experience, I was ready to quit.

After several heart-to-heart talks with the remaining white members, and getting some feedback from my black congregants, it was apparent that things in our church had split right along ethnic lines. It was also apparent that other cultural issues (social class, gender, etc.) had played a role. While trying to figure out next steps, Acts 6:1-7 came alive to me.

One thing I don't like about "guru" books is a formula: "Just do x, y, and z and your ministry will experience phenomenal success!" I am *not* making such a claim with what I am about to share. Quite simply, here are principles that have worked for me in three types of Christian organizations (church, university, and denomination) and may work in your context.

Principle #1: Truth-telling

Within this community of believers, we see a reconciliation issue on the table. The converts, who were of Greek ethnicity (Grecian Jews), were feeling a bit of injustice. From their cultural seat in the stadium, it looked as if their widows in poverty were not having their needs met. They brought this matter to the church leadership, which at the time happened to be made up of all Hebrew Jewish converts. Both groups communicated what they observed and needed, and the community came to a meeting of the minds.

It's a huge step forward to speak the truth, to navigate honest discussions about where you and your ministry community members live culturally and where those cultures intersect.

One evening, just before an important event where I was to deliver a presentation my wife, Caroline, grabbed me backstage and whispered, "Your fly is open." With her help, I discreetly prevented an embarrassing situation of everyone knowing what type of underwear I was wearing!

What if she hadn't told me the truth? I would have been on stage and the crowd would not have heard a word I said. They would have been either too busy laughing or too uncomfortable to even look at me. She cared enough about me to tell me the truth. With people we truly care about, we're honest about what matters, regardless of how uncomfortable we feel.

To achieve reconciliation we must break the Christian ritual of politeness and be honest concerning cultural issues, no matter how painful or uncomfortable the situation.

Every week, Christians practice the art of "slightly" lying to each other, which I call the ritual of politeness. As a straight shooter, let me ask some basic questions to see if you have participated in this ritual.

How many times have you told a preacher, "That sermon was fantastic" when it wasn't? Or complimented the worship leader and then, on the drive home, told your spouse how off-key his or her singing was? How many times have you told someone, "Great dress" or, "Sharp tie" when really you were thinking, *Wow, I'd never wear that.*

Of course, telling little white lies on trivial things such as these is not earth-shattering. In fact, I already know the standard defense: It's the "Christian" thing to do, because you didn't want to hurt the other person's feelings.

I contend, however, that for most people, politeness is not the real reason they skirt the truth in their relationships. I believe that most people want to protect themselves from conflict.

This natural reluctance must be overcome if your ministry is going to make serious strides. In many cases, the fear of being uncomfortable is what most hinders reconciliation efforts.

We must own the fact that if we refuse to speak the truth because of fear, we are operating as hypocrites. We may be polite hypocrites, but still hypocrites. Let me give you three different scenarios, and then I'll explain what they have in common:

Far too often I hear, "Alvin, I don't see you as a black man; I just see you as a man."

My friend Liza laments when men tell her they see her as a colleague because she "acts like a man."

And young, millennial-generation leaders tell me how sick they are of hearing about how they "will grow out of it" when they try to bring new ideas to the table.

With these examples I'm not talking about politically correct semantics — it goes deeper than that. Remember that language shapes how we view reality and it reveals values. When someone tells me they don't see my skin color; tells Liza that her worth as a woman is dependent on her acting like a man; tells a millennial leader that his or her ideas are wrongheaded simply because of age, that person's language reveals a disconnect with biblical truth.

Didn't God create the different ethnicities in a way that we should notice? Didn't God make two distinct genders with different characteristics, on purpose? Does not the Bible tell us, "Don't let anyone look down on you because you are young, but set an example for the believers in speech, in life, in love, in faith and in purity?" (1 Timothy 4:12)

When potentially offensive situations such as this arise, we have two choices: We can be polite and pretend nothing happened; or we can tell the truth, work through the issue, and aim to find common ground.

If I, Liza, and these young leaders are to practice a lifestyle of truth-telling and open conversations that might truly lead to reconciliation, we might forthrightly (yet calmly) reframe the comments we received in this way, offering grace to what offends us rather than ignoring it:

Alvin, I don't see you as a black man; I just see you as a man. — "I appreciate that you want to minister alongside me. At the same time, God made me both black and a man, and I don't want to deny what God made me. So maybe we should talk about what you are really trying to tell me, so that we are on the same page..."

Liza, you're one of us for sure. Thanks for acting like a man in that meeting and putting that guy in his place. — "You know what? I would really like to discuss what you mean by that. It sounds as if you may be saying that you want women to lead like men and, well, since God made me a woman, I don't think that is possible. Let's unpack what you just said to me..."

Interesting idea, Paul. Now, once you get older, it'll become clearer what works best in this situation. — "I'm not sure I understand what exactly about my idea you think won't work? It sounds as if you're implying that because of my age my idea has no merit. Why do you think that?"

Practicing successful reconciliation depends on living a truth-telling lifestyle that reflects God's reality of living in a broken world of cultural assumptions. As we practice reconciliation we must keep this reality in mind.

Principle #2: Providing dignity for all

All cultural groups need to be treated with dignity. In our Acts 6 example, everyone was considered one and the same, i.e. equal partners. Notice that both ethnic groups (Hebraic and Grecian Jews) anticipated and recognized equal status in dealing with the cultural tension of the situation. Equal status within the situation cannot be underestimated.

One killer of reconciliation efforts is paternalism — the intrusion of one group on another against its will. The intrusion is justified by a claim that the group intruded upon will be "better off." What results is a one-sided relationship.

As a former urban pastor, here is what paternalism looked like for me: At Christmastime I used to field phone calls from suburban pastors who wanted to donate clothes and toys to my former ministry. As much as I appreciated their goodwill, my standard answer was, "No, thanks. What I really need are women willing to build relationships with some of our single moms. I need tutors for kids. I need people who can have our folks over for dinner and vice versa in order to break down barriers."

After hundreds of conversations along those lines, I am sad to report that only two churches ever took me up on my counteroffer. Unlike the church leadership in Jerusalem represented in Acts 6, most churches were not interested in a partnership that benefited all involved. Those suburban church leaders were only interested in meeting their needs of playing Santa Claus at the cost of devaluing my church's needs.

One of the ways that dignity is provided for all is that *everyone has unified goals outside of reconciliation*. In the Acts 6 passage, the goal was not reconciliation. The goal was to make sure that all of the widows, regardless of ethnic background, were served properly. Reconciliation was a byproduct.

My job as director of reconciliation in the Evangelical Free Church of America came about via EFCA leaders practicing an active, goal-oriented effort *not* initially focused totally on reconciliation. The process unknowingly started when the leadership created a new mission statement which reads: "to glorify God by multiplying healthy churches among all people."

After a number of years, senior leadership realized that reconciliation must occur if we are to reach our mission goal, which then led to my hiring.

Principle #3: Developing interdependent partnerships

Within the world we live, conflict often manifests itself through cultural group competition. Ethnic groups vie against each other for political power; genders jostle over ideology within the university; corporations and governments displace poor residents by gentrifying neighborhoods; the list is endless.

Within Christian ministries, achievement of goals must be an interdependent effort without competition. Simply put, the philosophy should be "give me everything and I'll give you everything." It is apparent in the Acts 6 passage that everything was on the table in order to solve the problem and reach the common goal.

The Hebraic Jews did not limit the list of possible solutions in order to protect their own interests. This led to them handing over leadership of the entire food distribution ministry to the Grecian Jews (notice that all the names of the newly appointed deacons are Greek).

The Grecian Jews also did not hold a grudge, and there is no evidence that once they were in charge there was "payback" of any kind to the Hebraic Jews. What the church in Acts 6 experienced was an organizational restructuring so that both groups were dependent on each other for success.

At that meeting the organizational policies, practices, and procedures were changed in order for their organizational stakeholders to experience a "win-win" situation. After the board meeting, actions were taken that made clear the direction the church was headed. The results?

"So the word of God spread. The number of disciples in Jerusalem increased rapidly, and a large number of priests became obedient to the faith." I don't know how much more of a win you can have as a ministry leader.

Principle #4: Focusing on the long term

This principle is not necessarily found in the Acts 6 passage, but I think it is implied. After paternalism, the biggest killer of reconciliation efforts is a short-term focus. Practicing reconciliation with a short-term view ensures that there will be a "dandelion effect" on your ministry.

I live in Ohio and every spring, unless I fertilize, my lawn is invaded by dandelions. During the summer, fall, and winter, however, they are nowhere to be found. They pop up with ferocity in the spring, then fizzle out.

Reconciliation efforts in ministries usually follow the pattern of the dandelion in Ohio. People get excited, have events and programs, and for a season within the ministry, reconciliation is really hot. Things are popping everywhere. However, after some time has passed and the initial excitement has faded, reconciliation eventually fizzles out.

Leading with reconciliation in mind is not a one-time, seasonal event. It is not something requiring a few minor adjustments for everything to work fine. As with anything else of primary value, you must craft and plan in such a way that reconciliation is interwoven within the DNA of your ministry.

Some of those reading this book are an "Abraham," meaning that you will be the initiator of the gift of reconciliation. However, all you may see from your efforts is Isaac, or the beginning of change. It may be that whoever comes after you may actually reap the harvest.

In the book *Resident Aliens*, the authors tell the story of a pastor who had recently retired. He was invited to come back and preach at a church he had served for five years during the '60s. It was ironic that they wanted him to guest preach, because the years of his service had been stormy and difficult.

He had angered many people by encouraging the church to take a stand on a major issue of the times, desegregation. The church's neighborhood was changing demographically, and instead of leaving, he had felt they should reach their new neighbors. Eventually it became too much and he moved on. To his astonishment, when he entered the church 20 years later, he saw an integrated congregation!

When implementing reconciliation, I liken it to what Paul reflected in 1 Corinthians 3:6: "I planted the seed, Apollos watered it, but God made it grow." Your role might be to plant the seeds of reconciliation. Or to water them. Or to make them grow. At River of Life I watered; at Cincinnati Christian University I planted the seeds; in my present position at the EFCA, I am helping them grow. Regardless, you must keep the faith that God is with your efforts.

Reflection & Action:

Before we can effectively incorporate these principles of living in a globalized world, we need to gain a balcony perspective on our ministry community. (Remember, ministry community refers to the people who form their lives together within the context of your ministry.) The following questions are meant to take you to the balcony and help you identify the mainstream culture at work within your ministry community:

1. To determine your mainstream culture, start first by obtaining demographic data concerning your ministry community:

   • Race/ethnicity
   • Social class
   • Gender
   • Age/generation

2. Next, evaluate which group in each of those four categories is the largest. Your mainstream culture will usually mirror the values,

attitudes, and beliefs of the higher percentage of each group represented within your organization.

3. With your mainstream culture in mind, examine the following descriptions. Which best represents your current ministry community? [1]

Exclusive/Passive View
> • Intentionally excludes or segregates certain groups of people from the mainstream community culture.
> • Systematically resists cultural change through the formalization of policies, practices, and procedures that ensure separation; will not consider modification.
> • Will tolerate a small number of people outside the mainstream community culture who assimilate easily; however, these people hold no positions of leadership.

Symbolic/Paradigm Shift
> • Begins a public process of events that shows intent to embrace reconciliation (diversifying staff, public apologies for past actions, creating diversity committees, etc.).
> • Desires to open the community doors to people outside the mainstream culture of the ministry community.
> • Begins modifying policies, practices, and procedures with reconciliation in mind.
> • Assimilated groups of people outside the mainstream community culture are given limited leadership positions.

Structural/Incarnational Change
> • Modifies all policies, practices, and procedures to ensure full participation of people regardless of cultural background.
> • Commits to the process of intentional community restructuring to accommodate diversity and is willing to endure the potential political and financial fallout.
> • At least 20 percent of people outside the mainstream

---

1. Chart & explanations modified form *Continuum on becoming a multi-cultural church* by Crossroads Ministry.

community culture are members of the community and hold positions of influence on all levels of the leadership structure.

Transformative Steps

Cultural issues seen as deficits	Tolerance of cultural issues	Cultural issues seen as assets
1. Exclusive View: A Segregated Community	3. Symbolic Shift: An Open Community	5. Structural Change: An Integrated Community
2. Passive View: A Tolerant Community	4. Paradigm Shift: An Awakening Community	6. Incarnational Change: A Transformed Community

4. Discuss the following questions:

• What's keeping us from taking the next step?

• Any biblical disconnects in these reasons?

• If we take the next step, what must I change about my perspective as a leader? What must our ministry community change?

• If we take the next step, what are the losses involved? What do we gain?

Conclusion

I began by telling you not to expect to find all the answers to practicing reconciliation in this small guide. But I hope that I have helped you at least pull together some principles that will enable you to lead with reconciliation in mind:

1. Essentially, there are two significant assumptions underlying the conversation about reconciliation in the Christian world today that must change: (1) it's not necessary, and (2) it only concerns black/white racial issues. Both ultimately hinder rather than help reconciliation efforts, and unless we reshape the way we think and act, we will not take significant steps forward in a globalized world.

2. The journey of reconciliation begins within. You can't lead anybody anywhere that you haven't been yourself. Reconciliation cannot be faked. It is not a trendy new technique to be more in tune with the culture. It is an expression of God's work within you.

3. When it comes to reconciliation, the first step of the church in a deeply broken world is not strategy, but prayer. You will not be successful unless you develop a vibrant, strong prayer life.

4. What makes looking at our lives and ministries through culture so powerful is that it gives us the ability to organize our experiences on common ground — to speak a common language that matches the globalized world in which we live.

5. Typically, secular diversity is pursued as the end goal — an accomplishment, and/or an experience to be gained. This is not the case for believers. Reconciling people is about gaining Christ's point of view toward them, regardless of how different they are from you.

Five Frequently Asked Questions

What is reconciliation?

Reconciliation is God's initiative, restoring a broken world to His intentions by reconciling "to Himself all things" through Christ: the relationship between people and God, between people themselves, and with God's created earth. Christians participate with God by being transformed into ambassadors of reconciliation. - *Duke Center for Reconciliation*

Why is reconciliation important?

Christian motivation is primarily theological. We believe that reconciliation is the mission of God in our broken world. The Great Commission will be fulfilled by living out the first and second greatest commandments (Luke 10:25-37).

In order to successfully reach their mission, ministry communities need to intentionally create an accepted framework to define reconciliation, track progress, and create systems of accountability that will facilitate transformation.

I get what you're saying on the black/white stuff. But in our area it still is a black/white racial divide that dominates. What can my ministry do?

Remember that you can get to the race issues by framing the discussion in theological reflection and cultural adaptation. We have to get people to see each other as people while respecting differences, without an "us vs. them" mentality. If you don't, you run the risk of your efforts turning into an exercise in endless social analysis, followed by polarization, ending in bitter and hurt feelings.

My community is not racially or ethnically diverse at all. How does reconciliation affect me?

Reconciliation is not just about racial and ethnic dynamics. *Every* ministry context has groups of people that are "in" and groups that are "out." As leaders, to spur our ministries to maturity, we need to spearhead the building of relationships to whatever the out-groups are within our sphere of influence.

We are at ground zero. How do we get started?

There is no one-size-fits-all answer. However, I will share one tip, because it will help you go somewhere (where, only God knows!):

Just do something; anything.

You will make mistakes, and there will be heartache. But you can't get to your destination if you don't start walking.

Find what is commonly being called a "third place." These are places between home and formal institutions. However, make sure this third place has the group(s) you desire to reach in it. An example is a coffee shop. One common third place where many ministries start their journey is schools. Schools are formal institutions, but things like after-school programs and sporting events may contain the characteristics of third places. Many start by tutoring and/or mentoring out-group kids.

Really, anything that will get you and your ministry community building positive relationships with people different from you will begin your journey. And use this handbook to manage the harvest! May God bless you as you attempt to build something difficult and significant within the community of people you are called to lead.

Afterword

In the mid 90s, eighty leaders of the Evangelical Free Church of America (EFCA) from across the spectrum of the denomination met in a series of summits to discuss the EFCA's future. Many positive results flowed out of those discussions, the most profound being the establishment of a new mission statement: "The EFCA exists to glorify God by multiplying healthy churches among all people."

At the time, none of us fully grasped the impact of that statement on a historically northern European movement. While still majority Anglo, the EFCA is now about 15% non-white, and the most recent church planting statistics show that ministry at 25% non-white.

The statistics above only scratch the surface as to why the manual you're holding is important as a first step in providing resources for the journey of reconciliation. It is necessary to understand that reconciliation is a long journey with the implications of metaphor kept in mind.

This journey is critical because reconciliation is at the very core of the Father's plan. In Christ, He is about the business of reconciling the world to Himself. The church is failing to fulfill His plan if all believers are not reconciled to each other.

When Paul talks about the barriers being demolished at the cross, he is not just referring to our access to God, but also the transformation that must take place in the way we relate to each other across racial/ethnic, gender, generational, and social class divides.

Starting the journey, however, must include recognition that we need tools and resources. This journey is a long and winding road. We may at times feel like our progress is slow or even negative. But it is critical that we stay on the journey for the fulfillment of the Father's call on our lives.

In 1963, a 16-year-old boy who had grown up in a racially prejudiced rural culture heard Dr. Martin Luther King Jr. give his "I Have a Dream" speech. Something resonated deep in my soul, connecting with what I had learned from studying the Bible since early childhood. The journey for me began!

Most days I feel like I've just begun until I look back and see that progress in my life. Thankfully there have been several guides for the journey, including the author of this manual. After your first encounter with this material, where are you on the journey?

Have you begun? How about the ministry you lead? Are you willing to invite others to join you? Though difficult, the journey is exciting, challenging and rewarding. But more importantly it is biblical and at the heart of the Gospel.

Dr. William Hamel
President, Evangelical Free Church of America